THE WORLD OF DRAGONS

REAL-WORLD DRAGONS

BY MATT DOEDEN

CONSULTANT:
BARBARA J. FOX
PROFESSOR EMERITA
NORTH CAROLINA STATE UNIVERSITY

CAPSTONE PRESS
a capstone imprint

Blazers Books are published by Capstone Press,
1710 Roe Crest Drive, North Mankato, Minnesota 56003
www.capstonepub.com

Library of Congress Cataloging-in-Publication Data
Cataloging-in-publication information is on file with the Library of Congress.
ISBN 978-1-62065-146-9 (library binding)
ISBN 978-1-4765-1376-8 (ebook PDF)

Editorial Credits
Aaron Sautter, editor; Kyle Grenz, designer; Eric Gohl, media researcher;
Jennifer Walker, production specialist

Photo Credits
Capstone: Jonathan Mayer, cover; Corbis: Sam Forencich, 14–15; Jon Hughes: 11, 12–13; Newscom:
Mirrorpix/Daily Mirror Sidey Arthur, 18–19; Shutterstock: Clara, 20–21, IVP, 27, Joe Belanger, 24–25,
kkaplin, 8–9, Kostyantyn Ivanyshen, 6–7, Marcio Jose Bastos Silva, 4–5, Stu Porter, 26, Tristan Tan,
28–29, Unholy Vault Designs, cover (background), 1, Uryadnikov Sergey, 22–23, Victor Habbick, 16

Design Elements
Shutterstock

Printed in the United States of America in Brainerd, Minnesota.
092012   006938BANGS13

TABLE of CONTENTS

IT'S A DRAGON!

Two villagers are traveling in the mountains thousands of years ago. They discover some dinosaur bones. But they don't know what kind of beast the bones are from. One of the villagers cries, "It must be a dragon!"

DRAGON FACT

Ancient people did not know much about animals and nature. They often made up stories about dragons or other monsters to explain what they saw.

When ancient people saw dinosaur **fossils**, their imaginations likely ran wild. Today's dragon **myths** may have grown from the stories told by these frightened people.

fossil—the remains or traces of an animal or a plant, preserved as rock

myth—a story told long ago that many people believed to be true

Today we know dragons aren't real. But some real-life beasts look like dragons. The bones of prehistoric animals and some current animal **species** remind us of dragons.

species—a group of animals with similar features

frilled dragon

PREHISTORIC MONSTERS

Dinosaurs are easy to mistake for dragons. Tyrannosaurus rex was one of the largest **predators** of all time. This huge beast grew up to 20 feet (6 meters) tall. It also had 7-inch (18-centimeter) teeth.

predator—an animal that hunts other animals for food

DRAGON FACT

The name tyrannosaurus rex means "king tyrant lizard."

Pterosaurs were large flying **reptiles** that lived with the dinosaurs. Some had **wingspans** up to 40 feet (12 m). Most had long, narrow heads and small, sharp teeth.

reptile—a cold-blooded animal that breathes air and has a backbone

wingspan—the distance between the tips of a pair of wings when fully open

Dragons in most stories also have large wings and sharp teeth.

LIVING LEGENDS

Dinosaurs died out millions of years ago. Yet stories about dragons are found in **cultures** all over the world. Could some prehistoric creatures have survived into recent times? If so, people might have mistaken such animals for dragons.

culture—a people's way of life, ideas, customs, and traditions

Loch Ness monster

DRAGON FACT

The coelacanth is an ancient fish that was once thought to have died out. But several have been found since 1938. Perhaps ancient sailors thought this large fish was a sea dragon.

plesiosaur

People have reported seeing Scotland's Loch Ness monster for hundreds of years. There is no proof that the creature is real. But it may have led to some old dragon legends from Scotland.

DRAGON FACT

Plesiosaurs were large swimming reptiles. They lived alongside the dinosaurs. Some people think the Loch Ness monster might be a surviving plesiosaur.

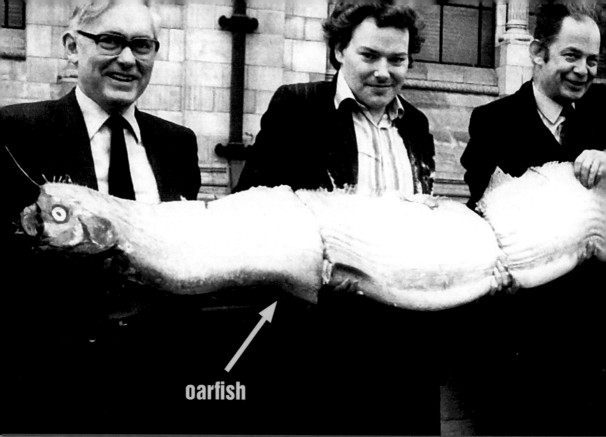

oarfish

Ancient sailors often told stories about their lives at sea. They didn't know much about ocean animals like oarfish or giant squid. People may have thought these creatures were huge sea dragons.

DRAGON FACT

Giant oarfish often grow up to 50 feet (15 m) long.

TODAY'S DRAGONLIKE CREATURES

Several modern animals remind people of dragons. Alligators and crocodiles have long jaws filled with jagged teeth. They also have long tails and thick, armorlike skin.

Chinese alligators have long, thin bodies. They look very similar to pictures of dragons from China and Japan.

American alligator

21

DRAGON FACT

About 50 kinds of deadly bacteria live in the mouths of Komodo dragons.

Komodo dragons are the largest lizards in the world. They have sharp claws, razor-sharp teeth, and a **venomous** bite. Komodos easily remind people of fierce dragons.

venomous—having or producing a poison called venom

Giant Pacific salamanders have long, flexible bodies and tough skin. Some Asian dragon stories may be based on these animals.

Some sea creatures look like dragons. Leafy sea dragons get their name from their dragonlike appearance. Dragon moray eels have mouths full of sharp teeth.

dragon moray eel

25

The sky is also filled with animals that have dragonlike features. People may think of dragons when they see large vultures soar overhead. Large dragonflies may also bring dragons to people's minds.

Some large dragonflies can fly faster than 20 miles (32 kilometers) per hour.

bearded dragon

DRAGON FACT Some dragonlike animals are kept as pets. Lizards such as frilled dragons and bearded dragons are popular pets.

People have told dragon stories for thousands of years. Dragons aren't real, but people still enjoy imagining them. Everywhere people look, real creatures remind them of fire-breathing dragons.

GLOSSARY

bacteria (bak-TEER-ee-uh)—very small living things that exist all around you and inside you; some bacteria cause disease

culture (KUHL-chur)—a people's way of life, ideas, customs, and traditions

fossil (FAH-suhl)—the remains or traces of an animal or a plant, preserved as rock

myth (MITH)—a story told long ago that many people believed to be true

plesiosaur (PLEE-see-uh-sohr)—a large swimming reptile that lived during the time of the dinosaurs

predator (PRED-uh-tur)—an animal that hunts other animals for food

reptile (REP-tile)—a cold-blooded animal that breathes air and has a backbone; most reptiles lay eggs and have scaly skin

species (SPEE-sheez)—a group of animals with similar features

venomous (VEN-uh-muhs)—having or producing a poison called venom

wingspan (WING-span)—the distance between the tips of a pair of wings when fully open

Read More

Riehecky, Janet. *Komodo Dragons: On the Hunt.* Killer Animals. Mankato, Minn.: Capstone Press, 2009.

Miranda, Edward C. *The Truth about Dragons and Dinosaurs.* Sarasota, Fla.: Peppertree Press, 2007.

Welch, Laura. *Dragons: Legends & Lore of Dinosaurs.* Green Forest, Ark.: Master Books, 2011.

Internet Sites

FactHound offers a safe, fun way to find Internet sites related to this book. All of the sites on FactHound have been researched by our staff.

Here's all you do:

Visit *www.facthound.com*

Type in this code: 9781620651469

Super-cool stuff!

Check out projects, games and lots more at
www.capstonekids.com

INDEX